Natural
wonders
of the world

WHITE STAR PUBLISHERS

CONTENTS

1
The archipelago of Maldives is made up of 1,190 pieces of land in a chain of 26 coral atolls.

2-3
Winter view of the Merced River in Yosemite Valley, in the western part of the Sierra Nevada.

TEXT
SIMONA STOPPA

GRAPHIC DESIGN
PAOLA PIACCO

INTRODUCTION

Photographed from space, planet Earth both fascinates and mystifies. An aerial view clearly shows that it is divided into oceans and continents; the shapes of North Africa and Arabia, the polar icecaps, the masses of clouds circulating in the atmosphere are all easily distinguished. But what is not revealed is what the naked eye can see close-up, what is photographed by the explorative mind, or how the heart reacts when we are enchanted by the Wonders of Nature.

This book wishes to offer the reader a Pindaric flight over the most beautiful natural sites in the world, described and illustrated to be enjoyed, comfortably seated, while their mind travels far and wide, delighting in the spectacular natural phenomena offered by the different elements: ice, earth and water.

Because Mont Blanc, Everest, the Vatnajökull glacier and the Patagonian Andes

4
Monument Valley is a plateau of fluvial origin characterized by its rocky buttes.

5
The spectacular Victoria Falls are on the border between Zimbabwe and Zambia, about halfway along the course of the Zambesi River

are just some of the ice giants that open the doors onto the infinity of vast white and immaculate expanses.

The Sahara Desert, the Grand Canyon, the Yellowstone National Park, the desert around Ayers Rock and the Ngorongoro Crater are only a small taste of the feast for the eyes that the spectacle of nature provides for those with eyes to see – and a heart to feel. And the lagoon of Bora Bora, the Iguazu Falls, the Okavango Delta, Australia's Great Barrier Reef and the Hawaiian islands are only a few of the fluid wonders that nature deploys to proclaim its energy, or demonstrate its tranquility.

In short, a world tour of nature's most memorable phenomena which, even if you cannot reach out and touch them, will ensure you are moved by the intense creative force that pervades the whole world.

6-7
In the Rangiroa atoll, in the Tuamotu Islands, French Polynesia.

8-9
Mount Everest, on the border between China and Nepal.

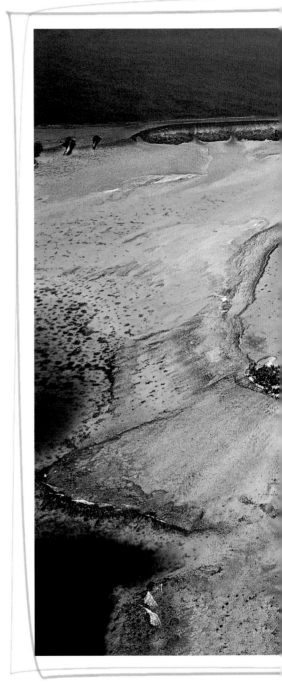

Chapter 1

THE FACE OF
THE WATERS

Where there's water, there's life. Hence these natural wonders: fluid, fresh, light, dynamic, suave, warm. Supple wonders that move: wonders with a soul. A land of majestic rivers and tempestuous torrents, with the Iguazu Falls and its leaping water, Latin America conquers the heart of anyone who pauses to contemplate it. On the border between Brazil and Argentina, the vast watercourse of the Iguazu hurtles down from a wide circular amphitheater made of basaltic lava, approximately 230 feet (70 m) deep and 8,858 feet (2,700 m) wide, breaking up into more than 270 waterfalls, and generating a breathtaking spectacle. But the prize for absolute magnificence goes to the "Garganta del Diablo," and its crashing, thunderous 262 feet (80 m) drop.

Also plunging headlong into a void, the Salto Angel is the tallest waterfall in the world, measuring 3,212 feet (979 m) in height, including an uninterrupted drop of 2,648 feet (807 m) of falling water. Another natural wonder is to be found in southern Venezuela, in the Canaima National Park, an area of

10
The enormous cloud of water formed by the Iguazu Falls; the rumble of the falls can be heard 13 miles (20 kilometers) away.

7,400,000 acres (30,000 sq km), dotted with Amazonian forests and tepuis – ancient massifs with sheer walls descending from a plateau. The waterfall, which is sacred to the indigenous tribes, is to be found along the Carrao River, and it cascades into the Kerepakupay River from the plateau of Mount Auyantepui.

But it is Niagara Falls – straddling the border between the United States and Canada – that deserves the title of "most famous waterfall in the world:" not for being the tallest, but because it is among those with the greatest volume of water: 212,000 cubic feet (6,000 cu m) per second. This drop of 184 feet (56 m) is caused by an overall difference of level of 328 feet (100 m) between Lakes Erie and Ontario. The Falls are divided into two sections: the American side, and the Canadian side, known as Horseshoe Falls.

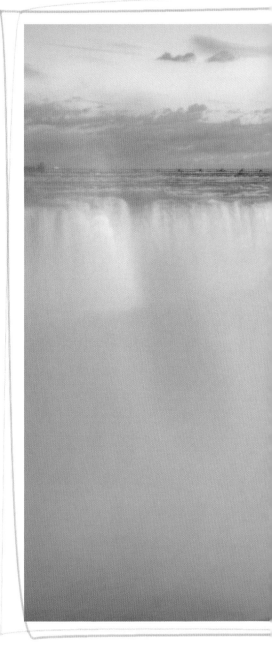

12
At 3,212 feet (979 m), Angel Falls, in Venezuela, is the highest waterfall in the world.

12-13
Because of their shape, the Niagara Falls on the Canadian side are known as Horseshoe Falls.

14
Kilauea is a shield volcano in the Hawaiian Islands.

15
The Na Pali Coast State Park encompasses 6,175 acres (2,499 ha) of land and is located along the northwest side of Kaua'i, the oldest inhabited Hawaiian island.

In the Pacific Ocean, approximately 1,800 miles (3,000 km) off the coast of San Francisco, the Hawaiian islands form an archipelago, a wonder of nature born of fire and water. Hawaii, the youngest of these islands, is nothing more than the emerging head of Mauna Kea, the highest mountain in the world, 33,474 feet (10,203 m) high, of which 13,796 feet (4,205 m) are above sea level. Hawaii, also known as "the island of orchids," is above all the island of the numerous volcanoes that brought it into being, and has a surface area of 1,600,000 acres (6,500 sq km). The second largest is the island of Maui, whose highest peak is Haeleakala (10,023 ft./3,055 m), an active volcano; mellow and romantic, this island offers 42 miles (68 km) of beaches, thus embodying the "American dream."

16-17
Bartolomé Island, in the Galapagos
Archipelago, off Ecuador.

17
The boobies of the Galapagos Islands can
be distinguished by their bright-blue feet.

The creative fury of fire also engendered the Galápagos Islands, an archipelago of volcanic origin off the coast of Ecuador consisting of 13 islands, 42 islets and 26 reefs, which inspired Charles Darwin's theory of evolution.

Almost entirely protected (97.5% is a national park), and declared a World Heritage Site in 1978, the Galápagos are home to 13 endemic species of sparrows, cormorants and giant tortoises, as well as the Galápagos iguana, the only species in the world that can live in the sea and feed on algae.

Another gem of the Pacific is French Polynesia, consisting of several groups of islands of volcanic and coralline origin. Polynesians sing "our land is the sea," as the 118 isles and atolls of French Polynesia are scattered across a marine surface as large as Europe. Standing out unmistakably

among the Society Islands is Bora Bora, "the pearl of the southern seas;" surrounded by a magnificent barrier reef, this isle is lapped by the most beautiful lagoon in the world, three times as large as its terrestrial surface.

18-19
Bora Bora, known as the Pearl of the Southern Seas, belongs to the Society Islands, in French Polynesia.

19
The Marquesas Islands are a group of volcanic islands in French Polynesia.

Along the north-eastern coast of Australia, across a surface of almost 86,500,000 acres (350,000 sq km), extends the crescent-shaped Great Reef Barrier, another natural wonder. This is not an unbroken formation but a collection of over 2,800 reefs including coral reefs, 618 continental islands, 300 madrepore

islands and over 200 atolls. It is the largest coral kingdom in the world, a habitat with over 400 species of coral, 4,000 species of mollusks, and 1,500 species of fish and shellfish.

20-21
The Australian Great Barrier Reef extends for over 135,000 square miles (350,000 square kilometers).

21
A sea fan ripples in the Ribbon Reefs, in Queensland, a coral barrier that boasts over 400 species of coral.

Africa too has some breathtaking aquatic surprises. "The river that never finds the sea" is the definition *par excellence* of the River Okavango. The third-longest African river (888 mi./1,430 km), it has no outlet to the sea, but gives life to the largest inland delta in the world, the Okavango Delta. Not far from the village of Shakawe, in Botswana, the River Okavango starts to branch out, its waters evaporating in the dry air and soaked up by

km) of which are protected by the Moremi Game Reserve; this oasis has the highest density of wildlife in the whole of Botswana.

An explosion of jets of water reminiscent of fireworks, Victoria Falls is on the border between Zimbabwe and Zambia, approximately halfway along the course of the Zambesi river. They owe their spectacular nature to the particular geographical setting: the river tumbles into a deep, narrow basalt gorge from an average height of 420 feet (128 m) and 1.2 miles (2 km) in width: a wonder enveloped in clouds of steam that rise over 1,640 feet (500 m) into the sky.

the sand of the Kalahari Desert, and finishing in the gigantic labyrinth of lagoons, canals and islands that form the delta, an alluvial plane of approximately 4 million acres (16,000 sq km), more than 1,200,000 acres (5,000 sq

22-23
Above the Victoria Falls, in Zambia, clouds of steam rise up to a height of 1,650 feet (500 m).

23
A herd of impalas in the Okavango Delta, the largest inland delta in the world.

Approximately 1,000 miles (1,600 km) off the eastern coast of Africa, the Seychelles archipelago features spectacularly eroded granite islands in the north and enchanting atolls in the south-west. Forty-six percent of these islands' terrestrial surface is under legal protection, while 88 square miles (228 sq km) of ocean are safeguarded by marine parks. The eco-islands of Curieuse, Cousin, Fregate and Bird are only some of the many bird-watching havens where the evolutionary dynamics of nature can be admired; while Aldabra – listed by UNESCO as a World Heritage Site because of its incredible biodiversity – merits the title of "the largest raised coral atoll in the world."

24-25
The granite beach La Digue at the Seychelles, an archipelago made up of 115 granitic and coral islands.

26-27
The Dead Sea marks out, situated about
1,300 feet (400 m) below sea level.

27
The saline concentration along the shore
of the Dead Sea, touches 33 percent.

Our journey now takes us to the Middle East, to visit the "sea which is not a sea," because it is not in fact a sea at all but rather a lake, situated between Israel and Jordan. This is the Dead Sea, found in the lowest depression on the surface of the Earth, at 1,312 feet (400 m) below sea level. 40 miles (65 km)

long and 3.7 to 11 miles (6 to 18 km) wide, its waters have a salt concentration of almost 33 per cent, 10 times that of the Mediterranean. The salinity of the Dead Sea has developed over a long period, thousands of years in fact, thanks to the Jordan and other rivers, whose waters, rich in salts "stolen" from the soil and rocks, have flowed into this gravity-defying terminal basin.

Our next destination is Europe, Norway, to be precise. Here is to be found the world's greatest concentration of fjords, steep-walled creeks, and sea inlets penetrating the coast for over 62 miles (100 km), to meander among the mountain ranges. Set in a wild and desolate landscape, Sognefjord is the longest

Norwegian fjord (127 mi./204 km). Above water level, the cliffs surrounding this long valley rise almost sheer to just under 2,000 feet (609 m), topped by a plateau from which towering mountains soar to 1,400 feet in height (1,370 m): a truly breathtaking spectacle!

28-29
The Norwegian fjords are characterized by their uncontaminated nature.

29
The Calanques stretch between Marseilles and Cassis, in France

The cradle of civilization, the Mediterranean is an intercontinental sea located between Europe, Northern Africa and Asia. Hosting large islands like Sicily, Sardinia, Corsica, Cyprus and Malta, as well as smaller ones like Capri and Ischia and countless Greek, Croatian, Turkish, French and Spanish islands, the Mediterranean is a middle earth that fascinates and intrigues with its colors and fragrances. As in Sardinia, with its fragrance of myrtle, its traditions and its breathtaking beaches. And as in Greece, with its famous islands, like the Cyclades, which are peaceful, quiet refuges, and its lesser-known ones, like some of those belonging to the Dodecanese group.

30-31
Navagio beach is a remote and
isolated bay on Zakynthos, in Greece.

31
The waters of Sardinia are a natural
paradise for sailors.

Chapter 2
THE THEATER OF THE EARTH

SAND DUNES, FORESTS, VOLCANIC MOUNTAINS, ENDLESS VALLEYS AND GIANT ROCKS: PARCHED IN THE TORRID LIGHT OF THE SUN, THESE ARE THE ELEMENTS OF NATURAL WONDERS SUCH AS THE SAHARA DESERT, "THE GREAT VOID" IN ARABIC. APPROXIMATELY 3,000 MILES (5,000 KM) LONG AND 1,200 MILES (2,000 KM) WIDE, STRETCHING FROM THE ATLANTIC OCEAN TO THE RED SEA, AND INTER-RUPTED ONLY BY THE NILE VALLEY. TRAVERSED BY THE TROPIC OF CANCER, THIS IS THE LARGEST DESERT IN THE WORLD AND ITS LANDSCAPES ARE AWE-INSPIRING: THE ERG, OR SEA OF SAND, WITH ITS SHIFTING DUNES; THE HAMADA, OR ROCKY PLATEAU; AND THE SERIR, OR GRAVEL-COVERED PLAIN – THE SAHARA IS AN INFINITE EXPANSE WHOSE HORIZON VANISHES IN THE INCOMPARABLE SHIMMERING LIGHT.

CONSIDERED THE THIRD EGYPTIAN DESERT – AFTER THE LIBYAN AND THE ARABIAN DESERTS, LYING RESPECTIVELY WEST AND EAST OF THE NILE – THE SINAI DESERT IS MADE UP OF IMMENSE EXPANSES OF SAND AND INHOSPITABLE MOUNTAINS. IN THE SOUTHERN REGION OF THE PENINSULA OF THE SAME NAME ARE TO BE FOUND ITS HIGHEST PEAKS: MOUNT CATHERINE (8,652 FT/2,637 M), THE HIGHEST MOUNTAIN IN EGYPT; AND MOUNT SINAI: ANOTHER *INFINITUM* THAT OPENS THE GATES TO TRANQUILITY OF SILENCE.

32
Saint Catherine's Monastery commonly known as Santa Katarina lies on the Sinai Peninsula, at the mouth of a gorge at the foot of Mount Sinai.

Still in Africa another natural wonder takes the breath away: Skeleton Coast, in northern Namibia. Despite its name – which refers to the remains of shipwrecks caused by the strong currents – it is truly spectacular: from the border with Angola, desert dunes of up to 1,000 feet (300 m) in height plunge for

310 miles (500 km) into the dark waters of the Atlantic Ocean. This is the coastal area of the Namib Desert, the wonderful "living desert."

34
Along the Skeleton Coast, the high dunes of the Namib Desert plummet into the Atlantic Ocean.

34-35
The Erg of the Sahara desert are characterized by shifting sand dunes, shaped by the wind.

36
The striking red calcareous karst in the Tsingy de Bemaraha National Park,
in Madagascar.

37
The extraordinary forest of karst pinnacles of Antsiranana, in Madagascar.

Declared a World Heritage Site by UNESCO in 1990, the Tsingy de
Bemaraha National Park is to be found in central-western Madagascar and is
another natural wonder. An immense forest of karst pinnacles, some of them
several hundred feet high, unfolds in a grid of perfectly straight lines. In this
natural reserve, the slow erosion of rainwater has left an astounding array
of traces in the limestone: labyrinths, clefts, subterranean caves, plunging
gorges and deadly sharp needles.

But Africa offers another delight: the "eighth wonder of the world," the Ngorongoro Conservation Area, also a UNESCO World Heritage Site.

Situated in the northeast of Tanzania, this crater is 7,218 feet (2,200 m) above sea level, and has a diameter of approximately 12 miles (19 km), the largest intact volcanic caldera on Earth. Thanks to its varied habitat, the crater

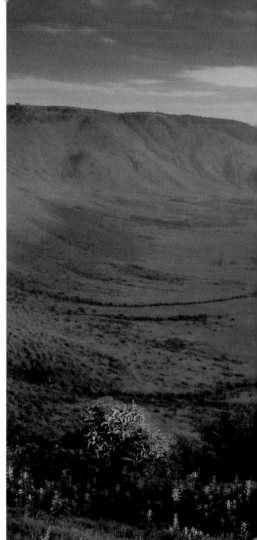

is a sanctuary for zebras and gnus, jackals, hyenas, baboons and hippos.

The innermost part of Ngorongoro is mainly savannah, occasionally broken by marshes, acacia thickets, and semi-desert zones; at its center, Lake Magadi, whose waters reflect the sky; while to the west lies

the immense Serengeti Plain.

This umpteenth wonder of the African landscape that makes us feel proud yet small at the same time is a region of 12,000 square miles (30,000 sq km), 80 percent in Tanzania and 20 percent in Kenya. The Serengeti Plain, which includes numerous protected parks, is

made up of prairies, savannah and woods, which provide the backdrop to impressive seasonal migrations. Approximately one-and-a-half million herbivores and thousands of predators are estimated to live on the plain: hence, this region resembles a sort of real-life Noah's Ark.

38
A lion in the savannah of the Serengeti National Park, which extends for about 5,790 square miles (15,000 sq km) between Tanzania and Kenya.

38-39
The west part of the crater of the Ngorongoro volcano, in Tanzania, is tinted with light colors at dawn.

Making our way to Asia we stop to be lured by the charm of southern Jordan's Wadi Rum, a spectacular desert valley that alternates rocks, mountains and sand dunes. Deep canyons, delicate natural arches and bridges, stones shaped like mushrooms by years of wind and erosion, in colors ranging from yellow to white, from red to brown, a

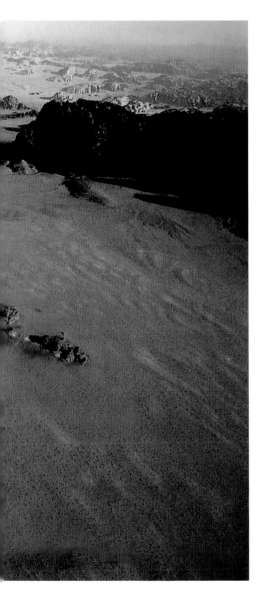

is largely steppes, with few species of thorny shrubs; at an altitude that varies between 2,960 and 8,200 feet (900 to 2,500 m) above sea level, it has temperatures of over 104°F (40°C) in summer and -40°F (-40°C) in winter. Its landscape is enchanting: rare expanses

harmonious, breath-taking palette.

Stretching across part of northern China and southern Mongolia over an area of 500,000 square miles (1,295,000 sq km), the Gobi Desert

of ochre-colored sand and dunes alternate with mountains and red-rock canyons, where dinosaur fossils have been discovered; and salt lakes, such as Orog Nuur and Böön.

42 and 43
Ayers Rock (left) is in the Northern Territory, while the Olgas (bottom left) are in the Kata Tjuta Park and the Pinnacles Desert (bottom right) is in Western Australia.

Each desert has its own distinctive characteristics. Located on the edge of the Nambung National Park in Western Australia, the Pinnacles Desert covers an area of over 42,000 acres (170 sq km): an expanse of ochre-yellow sand, dotted with thousands of pinnacles of up to 12 feet (4 m) in height, this unique desert has an otherworldly atmosphere.

Ayers Rock, Uluru for the Aborigines, is the most famous rock on Earth: 2.2 miles (3.6 km) long, 1,142 feet (348 m) high, and with a circumference of 5.8 miles (9.4 km), this enormous monolith of red sandstone is one of the natural wonders of the Outback of the Northern Territory in Australia. Ayers Rock provides one of the most exciting spectacles on the planet at dawn and at dusk: beneath the rays of the sun, this imposing rock transforms itself into a ruddy, fire-colored mass reminiscent of a flaming meteorite.

Just 22 miles (36 km) from Uluru lies another of Australia's natural wonders: Kata Tjuta, an Aboriginal term meaning "site of the many domes." This is known as the Olgas: a complex of 36 rounded monoliths forming a veritable labyrinth of fissured rocky domes and paths of incredible beauty.

The time has come to move to America, to enjoy – as if in a movie – a succession of natural wonders. The show opens with the imposing Grand Canyon in Arizona: 277 miles (446 km) of gorges and bastions, smoothed by the impetuous waters of the Colorado River. Ranging from 4,000 to 5,250 feet (1,200 to 1,600 m) in depth, its sides feature an amazing array of rock strata of different composition and color. The Grand Canyon has been a National Park since 1919, and a World Heritage Site since 1979. There are about 2,000 feet (365 m) of difference between the two sides: the South

Rim is mainly desert, while the more humid North Rim features conifer woods, poplars and birch trees.

In the south-west of the United States, in Utah, Bryce Canyon astounds with its expanse of needles and pinnacles of red, orange and white rock – the hoodoos – measuring 5.6 to 98 feet (1.7 to 30 m) in height. Formed from the erosion of sedimentary rocks by the waters of rivers

and lakes and the wind and frost, this natural spectacle is not a true canyon, but an enormous amphitheater set in Bryce Canyon National Park, established in 1928 – an astonishing American icon.

44
Bryce is distinctive due to geological structures called *hoodoos*.

44-45
The Grand Canyon is 277 miles (446 km) long, up to 18 miles (29 km) wide.

Located mainly in California, with a small part in Nevada, Death Valley is a large depression (150 mi./225 km long and 25 mi./40 km wide on average). Situated 282 feet (86 m) below sea level: it is a spectacular desert region of over 3,000 square miles (8,000 sq km) made up of dunes, mountain ranges, dry lakes

and numerous varieties of cactus and wildflower. Temperatures in this eerie and desolate landscape can reach 122°F (50°C), making it a truly "hot" wonder.

46
Saline formations in the depression of Badwater Basin, in Death Valley National Park.

46-47
The western United States, between Utah and Arizona, are home to Monument Valley.

48-49
A hot spring in Yellowstone National Park,
the oldest national park in the world.

49
The giant sequoias are the huge custodians
of Sequoia National Park.

Established in 1872, Yellowstone is the oldest national park in the world. Yellowstone – whose altitude ranges between 5,577 and 11,155 feet (1,700- 3,400 m) – covers an area of 3,468 square miles (9,000 sq km), comprising mountain ranges, crags, lakes, streams, waterfalls, forests, canyons and rivers. Here, earth, fire and water give rise to scenes worthy of Dante: pools of scalding mud;

scorching springs; the most numerous and spectacular geysers in the world.

A land of giants, the Sequoia National Park, in the southern Sierra Nevada in California, boasts majestic giant sequoia trees, and is home to five of the ten-largest trees in the world. Of all the park's giant sequoia trees, "General Sherman" is the largest living being on Earth, its summit leaves reaching a height of 311 feet (94.8 m). With a trunk diameter at the base of 36 feet (11 m), the "general" is thought to be over two thousand years old.

The Canadian Rocky Mountains – stretching between British Columbia and Alberta – hold a privileged position among the protected natural sanctuaries most valued by men. This mountain range takes in national and provincial parks, including Banff and Jasper National Parks; important glaciers, such as the Columbia Icefield; the "Cave and Basin" hot

mineral water springs; lakes, such as the Moraine, at over 4,900 feet (1,500 m) above sea level; and water courses plunging in thunderous waterfalls, such as the spectacular Sunwapta Falls.

50-51
A view of Lake Peyto and the Rocky Mountains, in Banff National Park in Alberta, Canada.

52
The Salar de Uyuni, in Bolivia, is the world's largest salt flat.

53
The Atacama Desert, in Chile.

South America also offers bewitching natural sites like Salar de Uyuni, for example, a salt flat of 4,633 square miles (12,000 sq km), situated on Bolivia's southern Andean plateau, at 11,975 feet (3,650 m) above sea level. With 11 billion tons (10 billion metric tons) of salt, and with 11 strata of thickness varying between 6.5 and 33 feet (2–10 m), Salar de Uyuni is the largest salt flat in the world. In northern Chile, between the Andean range and the Cordillera of the Pacific Coast, lies another natural wonder: the Atacama Desert. Shielded from humidity by the mountains, this is the driest desert on Earth, with an average yearly rainfall of 0.003 inches (0.08 mm), which explains its unique appearance. Though totally devoid of oases, this desert has pools of thermal water, altiplano lagoons, and the famous El Tatio Geysers, located at over 14,000 feet (4,300 m) above sea level, with water jets erupting to 26 feet (8 m) in height.

Situated in the southern part of South America, the Amazon Forest is the richest ecosystem on Earth, hosting approximately 60,000 species of plants, 1,300 species of birds, as well as 400 species of mammals and the same number of amphibian and reptile species, in an area of over 2,700,000 square miles (7 million sq km). This forest is penetrated for 3,902 miles (6,280 km) by the Amazon River. Fed by a thousand tributaries, this is the mightiest river on Earth. Approximately 65 percent of the Amazon's total surface area lies in Brazil, which boasts the largest primary forest in the world. In honor of what is considered to be the green lung of the planet, there is a Brazilian saying that states: "God is great, but the forest is even greater."

54-55
In Brazil, the Amazon rain forest is the richest and most complex ecosystem on Planet Earth.

Chapter 3

THE KINGDOM OF ICE

TO TALK OF ICE WONDERS IS NOT THE SAME AS TO TALK OF COLD WONDERS: BECAUSE OBSERVING A NATURAL WONDER IS ALWAYS A WARMING EXPERIENCE – AS ANYONE WHO HAS BEEN TO TIBET WILL TESTIFY. AN EXCEPTIONAL PLACE THAT RISES ON THE PLATEAU BY THE SAME NAME – THE HIGHEST IN THE WORLD – TIBET REACHES AN AVERAGE HEIGHT OF 16,000 FEET (4,900 M). COMPRISING MOST OF THE HIMALAYAS, THE TALLEST MOUNTAIN RANGE ON EARTH, TIBET FORMS A LARGE CURVE FROM NORTHERN INDIA TO SOUTHERN CHINA, WITH OVER A HUNDRED PEAKS EXCEEDING 23,950 FEET (7,300 M) IN HEIGHT, AND LEAVES VISITORS OPEN-MOUTHED.

AT 29,029 FEET (8,848 M) IN HEIGHT, MOUNT EVEREST – IN THE HIMALAYAS BETWEEN NEPAL AND CHINESE TIBET – IS THE TALLEST MOUNTAIN ON EARTH. THIS EVER-MOVING COLOSSUS OF ICE HAD BEEN A CONSTANT CHALLENGE FOR CLIMBERS SINCE 1921, AND IT WAS NOT UNTIL 1953 THAT THE SUMMIT WAS CONQUERED BY NEW ZEALANDER SIR EDMUND HILLARY AND THE NEPALESE SHERPA TENZING NORGAY, WHO REACHED THE PEAK FROM THE SOUTH FACE.

56
Mount Everest is the Earth's highest mountain, with a peak
at 29,029 feet (8,848 m) above sea level.

Also in Asia, straddling the border between China and Kashmir, the second-tallest mountain in the world, K2, reaches up into the sky to 28,251 feet (8,611 m). An imposing pyramid of rock and ice, K2 – which forms part of the Karakorum group in the Himalayas – had been the scene since 1909 of a struggle

between man and nature for the conquest of its summit: a feat achieved in 1954 by an Italian expedition led by Ardito Desio.

Mount Fuji, a volcano of 12,377 feet (3,776 m), is the highest mountain in Japan. A perfect colossal cone whose peak is covered in snow ten months a year, it is considered a symbol of Japan's natural beauty. Its last eruption dates back to 1707, and today this mountain is a gentle giant surrounded by five lakes at its feet and, in spring, fields of *sakura* cherry trees in bloom.

58
Mount Fuji, in the Hakone area,
is the highest mountain in Japan.

58-59
With its 28,251 feet (8,611 m), K2 is
the second-highest peak in the world.

Moving on to Russia, another natural wonder, Kamchatka, stands out: this peninsula of fire and ice, almost as large as Italy, is home to 29 active and 141 extinct volcanoes, all of them covered in wild forests. To the east, the most imposing volcano is the Kljucevskij, which reaches a height of 15,380

feet (4,688 m). But the unique aspect of this pristine and isolated region is the Valley of Geysers, a landscape of lunar charm with 42 large geysers, 22 of which are still active.

60
The crater of the Mutnovsky volcano, in Kamchatka, has numerous fumaroles and geysers.

60-61
Kamchatka, has 29 active and 141 extinct volcanoes.

Among the natural wonders of Europe, one of the most outstanding is the Vatnajokull Glacier, which covers one-sixth of Iceland. Almost 84 miles (135 km) long and 62 miles (100 km) wide, this colossus has an average thickness of 2,000 to 2,600 feet (600 to 800 m), and a peak of 3,280 feet (1,000 m) at its center. This enormous mass of ice conceals a heart of fire: it sits above a number of active volcanoes, including the Grimsvötn,

merizing natural wonder. Swedish Lapland, Europe's northernmost wild frontier, features a bewitching variety of landscapes: from the southern countryside and forests, through endless pristine expanses of tundra, great rivers and lakes, onto the hills that, towards the north, turn into an immense white desert, stretching towards the Arctic Ocean. In Lapland, as in other Arctic regions, it is possible to enjoy a wonder within a wonder: the amazing northern lights.

responsible for the perennial mist that envelops the glacier.

Comprising the northern zones of Norway, Sweden, Finland and the Russian peninsula of Kola, Lapland is another mes-

62-63
In Lapland, it is possible to view the Aurora Borealis.

63
The Vatnajokull glacier covers about 8 percent of the entire surface of Iceland.

64-65
With its 15,781 feet (4,810 m), Mont
Blanc is the highest mountain in Europe.

65
With its 10,968 feet (3,343 m), the Marmolada
is the Queen of the Dolomites.

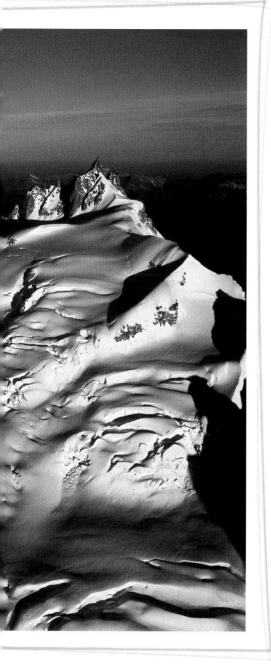

At 15,781 feet (4,810 m), Mont Blanc, on the border between Italy, France and Switzerland, is the highest mountain in Europe. Flanked by about 25 miles (40 km) of thrilling summits, from Col de la Seigne to Col du Grand Ferret, this massif is a veritable force of nature, scraping the sky with its incredibly sharp peaks – such as the Dent du Géant (13,156 ft./4,014 m in height) – and offering a breathtaking interplay of light and color.

In Italy we find another unique natural wonder: the Dolomites, the "mountains that blush." They owe this characteristic to dolomite, a sedimentary rock composed of calcium magnesium carbonate, which assumes blazing tones of pink and red at dawn and sunset. The Marmolada, the highest mountain of the Dolomites, with its 10,968 feet (3,343 m), is only one of the peaks of this range that stand out against the sky with their bizarre shapes and magical balance.

Moving on to Africa, we are captivated by the charm of Mount Kilimanjaro. At 19,340 feet (5,895 m), it is the tallest mountain on the continent. Located in north-east Tanzania, it is a mythical mountain for climbers, explorers and the indigenous peoples drawn by the pure-white snows that crown its peak. In fact, the Kibo Crater (15,430 ft./4,703 m) is covered all the way up in snow and ice, although it seems to be at risk of melting because of the greenhouse effect.

66-67
A large elephant against the backdrop of a landscape dominated by Kilimanjaro which, at 19,341 feet (5,895 m), is the highest mountain in Africa.

68
The peak of Cerro Torre, in the Southern Patagonian Ice Field –
between Chile and Argentina – is 10,262 feet (3,128 m) high.

69
The Torres del Pain National Park, in Chile, is home to the mountains
of the Cerro Paine range.

In South America we can admire the longest mountain range on Earth: the Andean Cordillera, stretching for approximately 4,750 miles (7,000 km) from the Isthmus of Panama in the north to Cape Horn in the south.

The Peruvian section of the Andean Cordillera, the Sierra, rises with imposing glacier-capped mountains reaching almost 20,000 feet (6,000 m) in height. Patagonia, in the extreme south of South America, offers breathtaking summits: among the most spectacular and inaccessible are Cerro Torre, standing at 10,262 feet (3,128 m), and Mount Fitz Roy, at 11,171 feet (3,405 m).

Dominated by the Patagonian Andes, this landscape varies from parched plateaus to primeval forests that turn into monotonous steppes that finally succumb to ice that ends up in the ocean. With the Perito Moreno Glacier, the Los Glaciares National Park is among the most astounding natural reserves of Patagonia.

70-71
The Andes form the mountain range of over 4,300 miles (7,000 kilometers) that extends from the north to the south of South America.

71
In Patagonia, the Los Glaciares National Park includes Argentino Lake, which is partly taken up with the Perito Moreno glacier.

72-73
An iceberg of King George Island, in the South
Shetland Islands, off Antarctica.

73
The Antarctic peninsula is covered with ice of
an average thickness of 7,200 feet (2,200 m).

At the southernmost tip of the continent lies the cold and inhospitable Argentinean province of Tierra del Fuego, with its lunar, wind-swept landscape. Its capital city is Ushuaia, the planet's most southerly city. This is the starting point for a journey to see

one of the natural wonders *par excellence*: Antarctica, the fourth-largest continent, situated south of the Antarctic Circle. An enormous, frozen desert, covered in ice 7,200 feet (2,200 m) thick on average, under which lie 145 lakes, interconnected by slow-moving glacial rivers. Antarctica is an infinite horizon which opens the doors onto the void, but it contains 90 percent of the planet's freshwater reserves.

At the opposite end of the Earth lies the Arctic, the region to the north of the Arctic Circle, around the Arctic Ocean, its ice pack, and the territories of Russia, Alaska, Canada, Greenland, Iceland and Norway. This is the "land of the midnight sun," so-called because here, from April to July, around the summer solstice, the sun sets around midnight. This surreal

phenomenon lends the landscape a magical, romantic quality. With its perennial glaciers, this region has winter temperatures of -72.4°F (-58°C), and summer temperatures between 14°F (-10°C) and 50°F (10°C). The climate of the Arctic is mitigated and regulated by the temperature of the seawater, which never drops below 28.4°F (-2°C), making this a "lukewarm" wonder of the world.

74 and 74-75
Midwinter in Lapland. Thick snow covers
the whole landscape.

76-77
Denali National Park in Alaska truly
is an expanse of snow and ice.

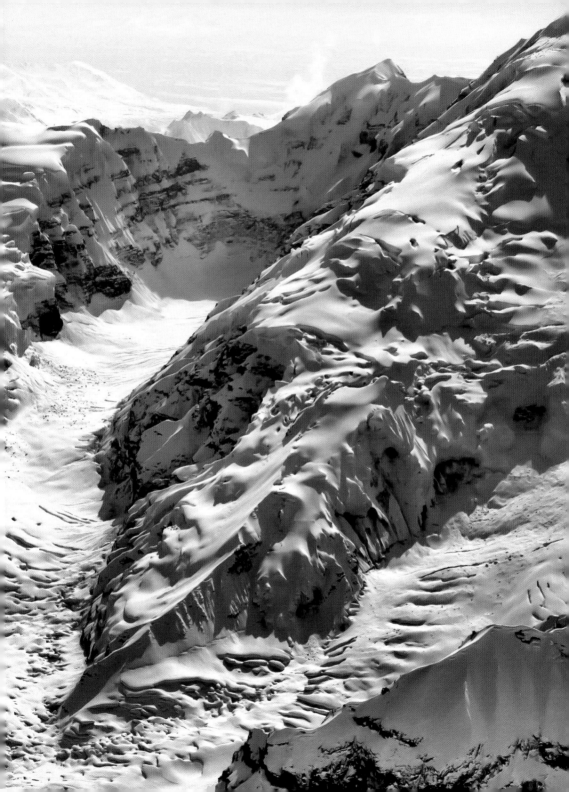

INDEX

PHOTO CREDITS

AUTHOR

Simona Stoppa a professional journalist, specializes in naturalistic, tourist, marine and anthropological themes. She is an author and writer of television formats of a documentary and journalistic nature and produces corporate films for a variety of companies. She writes for Touring Club Italiano and for Edizioni White Star, in addition to collaborating with various magazines and websites. She teaches television communication at the Università Cattolica in Brescia and is involved in corporate counseling with the use of audio-visual tools for the purpose of training paths in empowerment, team-building and teamwork.

WS White Star Publishers® is a registered trademark
property of De Agostini Libri S.p.A.

© 2013 De Agostini Libri S.p.A.
Via G. da Verrazano, 15
28100 Novara, Italy
www.whitestar.it - www.deagostini.it

Translation: Contextus s.r.l., Pavia (Sarah Jane Webb)
Editing: Contextus s.r.l., Pavia

ISBN 978-88-544-0805-0
1 2 3 4 5 6   17 16 15 14 13

Printed in China